101

DRESSAGE TIPS

Other books in the series:

101
DRESSAGE TIPS
Essentials for Training and Competition

Barbara Burn

The Lyons Press
Guilford, Connecticut
An imprint of The Globe Pequot Press

Copyright © 2006 by Morris Book Publishing, LLC

The Lyons Press is an imprint of The Globe Pequot Press.

10 9 8 7 6 5 4 3 2 1

Printed in the United States of America

ISBN-13: 978-1-59228-854-0
ISBN-10: 1-59228-854-5

The Library of Congress Cataloging-in-Publication data is available on file.

Contents

Introduction

My intention in writing this book is not to make you an Olympic dressage rider. (If I had that kind of expertise, I would be one myself!) I do hope, however, that the tips I have gathered from trainers and authors and teachers will help you understand some of the issues that face those of us who have chosen dressage as the way we want to work with horses. Many people start out in other disciplines—hunt-seat equitation, saddle seat, barrel racing, you name it—and gravitate toward dressage as they get older (and perhaps wiser). Some, like myself, learn to ride by the seat of their pants at an early age and spend years trail riding before learning what a diagonal is or how to get a horse to accept the bit.

In fact, I now believe that dressage should be the first discipline one learns as a rider, because it serves to improve virtually every horse regardless of his potential. I remember years ago discussing the virtues of dressage with a well-known jumper rider, who told me that he thought dressage would damage a good jumping horse by making it too collected (presumably giving it too much time to think about how high the wall actually was). But I noticed that he used many exercises that are part of basic training in dressage, which in the early stages is not about collection but about rhythm and straightness and all those other good things.

It is no coincidence that the term *dressage* comes from the French word that means training. The next time you watch a world-class horse and rider team perform piaffe or passage, don't think of these elegant movements as ends in themselves. Rather, think of them as means to an end—exercises that will encourage your horse to lower and engage his hindquarters and use his back properly to elevate the front end. The shoulder-in is not a trick to show off your horse's ability to do lateral work: it is a necessary tool to his learning how to balance properly, to strengthen his inside hind leg, and so on. An extended trot may dazzle onlookers, but it means nothing unless the horse also has a good working trot, a collected trot, and the ability to trot on a loose rein with his head lowered. In other words, what many think of as the goals of good dressage riding are actually milestones along the way that all dressage riders should attempt to master.

A Personal Note

You may wonder why someone like myself, an amateur novice rider rather than a professional teacher, would have the temerity to write a book with advice for others. But think of my role as a stand-in for yourself—someone to ask the questions, discover some answers by looking to experts, and put them into a format that is easy to use. This book is aimed primarily at amateurs who have not yet acquired a great deal of experience, but I have included a number of quotations from the great riding masters of the past and present. Their wisdom may serve as tips for more experienced riders and professionals to use in their work with amateurs.

The levade is one of the airs above the ground performed in the *haute école* (high school) of classical dressage. This is Bettina Drummond riding the Andalusian stallion Embajador XI. (photo: Gerald Incandela)

Part I

Getting Started

"The aim of this noble and useful art is solely to make horses supple, relaxed, compliant, and obedient and to lower the quarters, without all of which a horse—whether he be meant for military service, hunting or dressage—will be neither comfortable in his movements nor pleasurable to ride."

—François Robichon de la Guérinière

(photo: Mark Abelle)

Chapter 1

The Rider

Before one begins to teach, one must

learn as much as possible about the subject, and this is as true in training horses as it is in any other discipline. It is certainly possible to enjoy riding for its own sake without studying traditional techniques or horse psychology, but what is most rewarding about dressage is being able to ride a horse you have trained yourself. This requires some study on your part, not only by reading books but also by spending quality time in (and out of) the saddle, some of it under the supervision of an instructor.

tip 1. Trust what you know.

I am assuming that readers of this book know something about horses and riding, but perhaps not much about dressage. The first tip I would offer is to trust what you already know. Dressage may be a new discipline for you, one with a venerable history and specific training techniques and vocabulary, but it is not rocket science. If you have confidence in your abilities as a horse person, it should not be difficult to open your mind to some new ways of relating to your favorite animal companion.

tip 2. Bear in mind that dressage is about more than just riding.

According to de la Guérinière, the great eighteenth-century French master, "The knowledge of the nature of a horse is one of the first foundations of the art of riding it, and every horseman must make it his principal study." Although one cannot learn to ride by reading a book, one can learn a great deal about the horse and about training techniques from the great masters of both past and present. There are many books about horsemanship (the earliest known dates to the fourteenth century BC in what is now Turkey) and they vary considerably, depending on the experience of the author. Many are still worth reading (see recommended titles in Further Reading), in spite of the fact that they may take different approaches to the training of horses, just as trainers do. Consult these books on days when you cannot ride. One of the most rewarding aspects of reading books by the masters is coming across brilliant quotations like the one above; another is finding discussions of techniques that your trainer may not have had time to explain when you were in the saddle.

This etching by Jacques Callot (1634) shows King Louis XIII of France executing a levade in the battlefield, an excellent illustration of the aristocratic and military heritage of modern-day dressage.

tip 3. Study the history of dressage.

A phrase often heard in the world of dressage is *competitive versus classical*—as if the two were on opposite sides of the dressage spectrum. In fact, they developed from the same roots, beginning in Renaissance Europe when the classical form of training horses developed as an aristocratic pursuit based on the fourth-century BC writings of Xenophon, who described the training of horses for military use. During the nineteenth century, as trainer Jec Ballou describes it, "Dressage became less of an aristocratic pastime and moved into the cavalry schools . . . [where] equitation emphasized longer, flatter strides and greater adjustability of the horse's frame between varying degrees of collection." Dressage was traditionally performed in a small arena with Iberian horses that excelled in collection and agility; but by the time dressage became an Olympic sport in 1912, the size of the arena had been enlarged and fixed points established. The airs above the ground—the *haute école* of classical dressage—were largely dropped in competition in favor of extended gaits and precise movements. During the twentieth century, the so-called German school became dominant in competitive dressage, owing in part to the development of the larger, forward-moving breeds. Thanks to the teachings of such modern masters as Nuno Oliveira of Portugal, the French school of traditional classical training is re-emerging as a significant factor in contemporary dressage—even in competition, as judges increasingly acknowledge the distinctive quality of the Iberian breeds. In spite of their different approaches, however, the ultimate goal of each school is basically the same: to achieve what Alois Podhajsky, former director of the Spanish Riding School in Vienna, called, "the feeling that [the rider] is part of the horse—this is the aim of the classical art of riding."

tip 4. Don't be in a hurry.

Although one horse might have better conformation, talent, and attitude for dressage than another, his rider must not expect to achieve a high level of success without spending several years in the process. Not only must the rider learn to coordinate the use of his seat, legs, and hands, but the horse himself must learn to move in a balanced frame with a great weight on his back and to perform willingly and calmly under the precise control of the rider. And then the two must learn to work together as a team, in which (as teacher Erik Herbermann puts it) "the rider's mind does the thinking and the horse's body does the doing." Captain Etienne Beudant, in his 1950 book on horse training, cautioned his readers not to hurry the process when he wrote: "To observe and to reflect; these are the rider's surest means of success." In other words, take your time and think about what you are doing instead of rushing headlong toward Grand Prix!

On those days when you can't ride, curl up with a good book about training horses.

tip 5. Learn the language (French).

Not surprising, given the history of dressage, a large number of terms referring to different movements and stages in training have evolved over the years, most of them in French or German. Because the English translations are sometimes less expressive and less precise, it is worth learning a few phrases in their original language. For example, *rassembler,* the French term for collection, refers to the position in which the horse's hind legs are engaged, his back is elevated, and he is ready and able to perform instantly and energetically whatever the rider asks. As the word implies, *rassembler* is a bringing together of different elements. These include the *mise en main,* which describes the relaxation of the horse's jaw as he yields the bit to the rider, and the *ramener,* when the horse is flexed at the poll so that his nose reaches the vertical. *Descente de mains* describes the moment at which, when the rider relaxes his fingers, the horse remains in perfect balance.

tip 6. Learn the language (German).

The German training scale is definitely worth learning, as many trainers make it the foundation of their work. Based on the teachings of Italian, French, and German masters and adopted in the twentieth century by the German National Equestrian Federation, the training scale consists of six interdependent and progressive stages that culminate in collection: (1) relaxation (*Losgelassenheit*), in which the horse's muscles are free from tension; (2) rhythm (*Takt*), which refers to the regularity of the strides in each gait; (3) contact (*Anlehnung*), or acceptance of the bit (without the rider's pushing or pulling); (4) impulsion (*Schwung*), the energy created by the hindquarters and transmitted into the gaits; (5) straightness (*Geraderichtung*); and (6) collection (*Versammlung*), when the hind legs step well underneath the horse and take a greater share of the load in order to lighten the forehand and give more freedom to the movement of the forelegs.

Terms in English that express the meaning of *rassembler* and *Versammlung* include: acceptance of the aids, self-carriage, engagement, lightness, and throughness, which derives from the German word *Durchlässigkei,* or "letting the aids through."

tip 7. Learn where the legs are.

Ask your trainer or a knowledgeable friend to spend one or more sessions walking around the ring while you are on horseback, explaining where each leg is so that you will learn to feel when a hind leg is in the air (and when an aid will have some effect) or on the ground. Watching the horse's shoulders will enable you to determine which foreleg is moving forward, but you should eventually be able to feel the movement without looking. Trainer and author Sylvia Loch writes: "It may help if you think that when a grounded front leg passes the vertical, the hind leg on the same side is advancing in the air. Any rein action now will block the hind leg and force it to set down too early and the horse will not step under far enough."

Bonus tip: Read "The Mechanics of Movement" chapter in Stephen Budiansky's book *The Nature of Horses.* His explanation of how a horse moves at the different gaits will help you become the kind of rider who will help rather than hinder the horse—an animal that, after all, is capable of moving at speed and in perfect balance only a few hours after being born.

One of the most effective ways to develop a secure seat is to take a lunge lesson (or, preferably, many lunge lessons) with your instructor. (photo: Patricia Kuehner)

tip 8. Take many lunge lessons.

Ask your instructor or trainer to lunge your horse with you in the saddle. This is one of the most effective ways to develop a secure seat. Riders at the Spanish Riding School are trained on the lunge line without stirrups or reins for at least six months until they establish a secure seat, independent of the hands. Experienced riders return to the lunge line to correct any faults they may have acquired. With your mind free of worrying about your hands and the horse's direction or speed, you can concentrate on your own position in the saddle. You can also try various exercises, such as holding your arms above your head and turning right and left as you move around the circle.

One way to improve your seat is to watch a great rider, like Bettina Drummond on her mare Navoir. Note the position of the rider's legs, seat, and hands, and then envision yourself in the same pose. (photo courtesy Bettina Drummond)

tip 9. Think of your legs as blankets.

A number of trainers make use of imaging techniques to help riders feel the correct position for both themselves and their horses as they ride. One of the most effective images can be simply watching a great rider and trying to imagine what it feels like to be that rider. Or you can analyze your own body parts as different types of equipment.

For example, use your legs like blankets and drape them against the horse's sides. When you want to give a cue, press gently once (repeat only if the horse doesn't respond), but otherwise remain relaxed. Remember that a horse can feel a fly land on his skin and doesn't need you to kick or clamp your legs against his side to be aware of what you want. If he doesn't respond after a couple of tries, reinforce the aid with a light touch of the whip or spur, but don't nag with your legs.

tip 10. Understand the power of the seat bones.

English trainer Sylvia Loch often asks riders in her clinics to perform a simple exercise out of the saddle that dramatically demonstrates the effect the rider's seat has on the horse's back. Sit on your hands on a chair and feel your seat bones. Raise your upper body from the mid-section and allow your weight to drop into your legs. You will notice that your seat bones seem to disappear and your seat has become lighter. She says, "This exercise shocks a lot of people. Many have said that they never realized how much lighter it made their backsides in the saddle, when they have their feet under them and let their weight drop into their legs, supporting themselves upward. I wouldn't want them stretching up as much as they would for, say, passage. But just sitting tall, to walk forward or trot forward, they've found that quite incredible, especially the ones who think you have to push. When they go back and sit on a horse, they are amazed. Instead of pushing, they can sit very centered and just think 'light.'"

tip 11. Use your upper body to advantage.

Think of your upper body as an inflatable life-saving balloon allowing you to rise upward in the saddle. This will help the horse (and you) become light in front and to sit down behind. Imagine your back as a clutch. Bettina Drummond recalls that Nuno Oliveira "would go into the motion of the horse and redirect it. His back was like a clutch. He would ride the clutch and then ease it out in whatever direction he wanted. . . . The release of the legs was like riding the clutch against the accelerator, with the approach of the inside leg to incurve the horse and the outside leg to rock back the topline and collect it. The release of the inside rein and the approach of the outside leg deviate the course of the haunches to dominate changes in the horse's direction. Basically, the seat ruled the whole package and the release of the leg and hand aids expressed the package."

tip 12. Your arms and hands are not brakes.

Think of your arms as side reins attached at the elbow. Instead of pulling against the horse, move your shoulders back so that the horse is the one doing the pulling. Trainer Sally Swift suggests that you think of your arms as hoses through which energy pours from the hindquarters to the horse's mouth, rather than as restrictive devices.

The function of the hands, according to General Decarpentry, author of the classic manual *Academic Equitation*, is to "regulate the output in speed, the form, and the direction of the amount of impulsive energy produced by the horse." Nuno Oliveira puts it this way: "When I speak of the hands' action, I mean the opening and shutting of the fingers, giving way to the horse when he gives, and resisting firmly when he does not, never taking back on the reins, allowing the hand to resemble a filter."

tip 13. Take up cross training.

Since you cannot spend all of your waking hours in the saddle, put some of your spare time to good use by building up your own fitness, balance, and strength. Aerobic training is useful, but disciplines that emphasize balance, core strength, and coordination—such as yoga, tai chi, dancing, Alexander Technique, Feldenkreis, and Pilates—are even more valuable. One of the most important set of exercises you can do to help develop a secure seat is to loosen body blocks, stretch tight muscles, and develop weak abdominal muscles in order to stabilize your pelvis and upper body while allowing it to follow the horse's motion. German physiologist Eckart Meyners notes that "the correct seat is always in motion," and he believes that flexibility is more important than muscle strength.

This neatly turned-out pair is ready for a schooling session. Carol wears a helmet, gloves, and full-seat breeches and carries a regulation-length dressage whip; Lunar wears matching polo wraps and saddle pad, a snaffle bridle, and a dressage saddle. (photo: Kate Rudich)

tip 14. Dress the part.

Like other disciplines, dressage has a dress code. When schooling, however, you may dress as casually as you like—although a hard hat is always a must. Many riders like the security of suede full-seat breeches, often worn with half chaps and paddock boots (to save your good boots for competition). And don't forget gloves, which will not only protect your hands and give you a more secure grip on the reins but will also improve your communication with the horse by generalizing what your hands feel and what message they send to the horse. Spurs are used to reinforce your leg aids and not as punishment; but unless your trainer recommends their use, it is best to wait until you feel confident that your legs work independently and precisely. The whip can also be misused as punishment, but it is a basic aid reinforcing the leg, and all riders should learn to use one properly from the beginning. If you cannot move a whip from one side to the other without changing your grip on the reins, consider using two whips, one on each side. If you plan to compete, be sure your whip is no longer than the regulation 43.3 inches (including the lash).

tip 15. Practice without your horse.

Trainer Wendy Murdoch suggests that you use your time off the horse to practice aspects of riding with which you might be having trouble. "When it comes time to canter, I sometimes ask students to canter on the ground without their horse first. Almost all the mounted problems will show up when they canter solo, whether that is simply cantering straight or doing flying changes. I have found a certain percentage of students that could not canter at all. No wonder their horse has difficulty!" And she practices what she preaches: "I keep practicing all the movements over and over again in my head and on the ground. And I practice them perfectly, seeing the horse lightly move away from my aids, happy in his work, me sitting perfectly and smiling the whole time. And I understand the foundation of good movement in both horse and rider. If the foundation is sound, then performing the more advanced movements becomes easy."

Chapter 2

The Experts

"Instructors have different methods and different
lines. The pupil will only be able to judge the
standard after he has followed the teachings
loyally. So the first essential for every student is
to believe in his teacher unconditionally or else
leave the school. There is no halfway solution."

—Alois Podhajsky

These wise words from the former direc-

tor of the Spanish Riding School make it clear that selecting a dressage teacher is a major commitment, not to be taken lightly. Some
experienced riders will go from one clinic or trainer to another, pick-
ing up tips and ideas to incorporate into their own work; but for the
novice or for a rider new to the discipline, the choice of a teacher is
a very important first step.

tip 16. Get help.

First there is the riding instructor, who will teach the rider the basics; next there is the trained horse, who will enable the rider to feel the correct movements; then there is the trainer, who will teach the horse, using the rider as a medium; and then there is the coach, who will give intermittent help as needed on specific problems and perhaps in preparing for a show. Before buying a horse and engaging the services of a trainer, the prospective dressage rider must first learn the basics of riding—to develop a secure seat and to understand the aids and use them effectively. It is not enough to be able to ride on the flat; in fact, many riders who are experienced in other disciplines find themselves starting nearly from scratch when they take up dressage.

tip 17. Find help.

It is not always possible to find someone who is an expert horse trainer and also a gifted instructor, which is why it makes sense to "shop around" before making a decision. Go to dressage shows and watch the way instructors interact with their students—not during the tests, but during the warm-up period. Listen for encouraging words and a positive attitude, but also determine if the teacher has set up a plan for the warm-up and is paying attention to the student, rather than to a group of students. Talk to riders and get information about whether or not a particular individual is good to work with; then follow up by visiting facilities where you may watch clinics or lessons (be sure to call ahead to determine whether or not they welcome visitors). Once you have found an instructor you like, ask if he or she has time for you and offer to bring your horse to the facility for a lesson. If you do not have a horse, you will be expected to ride a school horse; this can be a tremendous advantage if the horse is well schooled.

tip 18. Develop a relationship with your trainer.

Trust and honesty are basic components of the bond between rider and instructor. As Olympic rider Lendon Gray puts it: "Just as trainers must be honest with their clients about their horses' abilities, instructors must be honest with their students about the students' abilities." And the student must be honest as well—about goals, ability to pay, and willingness to make a commitment. If your prospective teacher criticizes in a loud voice and you cannot deal well with that, make your feelings known—but be prepared to tolerate the criticism or look for another teacher. Although you may not know exactly what you want to learn, you should be clear from the outset as to your ambitions— whether that is to reschool your trail horse in dressage, or to improve your own riding skills. You may want help purchasing a suitable horse, or maybe you feel stuck in First Level and want to move on. Be prepared to sign a release if the instructor insists (often for insurance reasons) and be aware of your financial commitment. Some instructors charge by the lesson, with different rates for groups and individuals; trainers may charge a monthly fee or by session, with different rates for lungeing, schooling, or rider instruction.

tip 19. If necessary, make do.

If you cannot find or afford the instructor of your dreams, you may be able to progress by working on your own, attending clinics, reading good books and useful magazine articles, and watching advanced riders at other barns or at shows. And, of course, you should ask for help from someone you know who is a better rider than you are. Charles de Kunffy notes that, "Anyone a little ahead of another in riding experience or knowledge can be of assistance and useful as a teacher or helper of sorts, provided, of course, that with such an instructor no pretensions are made as to the possession of greater knowledge than is actually available. Little help is better than none." Ask a friend to make videotapes of you and your horse that you can study at home, or ask the stable manager if it might be possible to put up large mirrors at one end of the arena for you to consult as you ride.

One of the most important considerations in selecting a horse is the bond between horse and rider. Here the author shares a moment with her Lusitano friend, Maruxa. (photo: Mary Bloom)

Chapter 3

The Horse

As in many other equestrian disciplines,

the choice of an equine partner for dressage is a crucial one. Not only do we want a good athlete with the conformation, attitude, and physical ability that will enable the horse to learn the required movements and to perform them well, but we also want a partner with whom we can create a lasting relationship and a mutual respect. Many riders begin their adventures in dressage on school horses, where many of these traits are not readily apparent, and even many private horses are unsuitable for a career in dressage, so when time and finances permit, you may find yourself in the position to make that crucial choice.

tip 20. The advantages of a schoolmaster.

If you are a relative beginner, you should consider leasing or buying a schoolmaster, a well-schooled horse retired from competition. A horse that is well-mannered and forgiving of occasional mistakes can teach a novice the correct "feel" for the different movements. However, Alois Podhajsky cautions: "The school horse is a very important, almost indispensable assistant to the instructor. But he will be of full value only if the instructor is thoroughly acquainted with his movements and his temperament. . . . When the instructor has not trained the horse himself, he should ride the horse before starting to train his pupil in order to get to know his capabilities." Most dressage students, however, soon realize that working with school horses has its drawbacks. Dressage, after all, requires a bond between horse and rider, which is easier to attain if the horse works with only one rider who is responsible for all aspects of his care and training.

tip 21. Choose your horse to match your own ability.

The French trainer Jean Froissard suggests another approach: "You do not want an entirely green horse, which would require the employment of an experienced trainer if he was not to be spoilt. . . . Neither do you want a too highly trained horse, you would not speak or understand each other's language and the end would be the ruin of both of you. What you do want is a six- to seven-year-old having had as good and rational a basic training as you should have received." Don't fall for the "ready to ride" claims of breeders who advertise four-year-old horses that come fully equipped with piaffe and passage. Chances are these horses have been rushed into work far too early and pushed too far too quickly. Like true collection, these movements take years to achieve, and inadequate preparation can lead to sour behavior and physical problems, if not actual injury. The likelihood is that the horse will require rebreaking by someone who will allow the horse time to mature before making substantial demands on his body and brain.

tip 22. What breed is best for dressage?

There is no single "best" breed for dressage. When classical dressage was an aristocratic pastime, the Iberian breeds (Andalusian and Lusitano) were highly prized; indeed, the Spanish Riding School in Vienna still uses Lipizzans, which descended from Iberian stock. As dressage evolved into a competitive sport, larger, more forward-moving horses were developed to excel in dressage tests. Today, judges favor these European breeds (Dutch and Swedish Warmbloods and the German Hanoverian, Oldenberg, and Trakhener). But thanks to a revival of interest in classical training, Iberians are once again gaining acceptance in competition, especially at the higher levels. Because each breed has specific strengths, the selection of a trainer and a training approach will depend on the horse you choose.

Bonus tip: Many amateur riders shopping for horses with dressage potential look to breeders abroad instead of exploring the American market. European horses may be cheaper, but the cost of shipping a horse to the United States can run over $10,000. Another important consideration is that some European breeders break in their sales prospects quickly—installing "tricks" that will appeal to their customers, rather than taking the time to give the horse a good start.

With horses, beauty is not only skin deep, as conformation can also help a prospective owner determine whether or not a horse will be capable of performing. This photograph was taken in a breed class at a dressage show, where Maruxa was judged on her potential as a dressage horse. (photo: Patricia Kuehner)

tip 23. What to look for in a prospect.

There are many considerations in selecting a dressage prospect, including conformation, soundness, and attitude. A well-behaved horse, usually a gelding, is generally the right choice for a novice rider, but character is not everything. The physical capacity of the horse is determined by conformation, and a trainer and a veterinarian can be of invaluable assistance here (see tip 24). Educate your eye at breed shows and dressage competitions. Since dressage involves a willing partnership between horse and rider, however, it is very important that the rider sense a personal connection to the horse.

In addition to studying conformation, the prospective buyer should also look carefully at the horse's gaits at liberty. Here Maruxa shows off her powerful trot. (photo: Mary Bloom)

Bonus tip: Trainer Jean Froissard in his *Guide to Basic Dressage* offers excellent tips for selecting a potential dressage horse. Look for natural balance; never choose a horse "who stands higher behind than in front." Look for a relatively short back; observe how the horse carries his head and neck while trotting at liberty, and make sure his tail is neither too high nor too low, which might indicate stiffness. Examine the legs carefully for straightness, defects, and weaknesses.

tip 24. Get professional help.

No matter what kind of horse you plan to buy, be sure to ask a professional for advice at every step. First, you will need the help of a trainer who knows your own abilities and ambitions and can evaluate a horse's conformation and attitude in light of what the horse will be expected to do. It is appropriate to ask a trainer to review tapes or even to try out the prospective horse—a service for which you should provide a fee, as well as any traveling expenses. If the trainer finds you the horse, you may also be obliged to pay a commission.

When you find a likely prospect, ask a veterinarian to examine the horse and to review X-rays for unsoundness or weakness. Dressage may not seem as demanding on a horse's constitution as combined training or open jumping. But, in fact, dressage movements can be very wearing on the stifles, hocks, and back—especially with horses that have not been sufficiently schooled or warmed up—and a horse with congenital weaknesses may not be the best choice.

tip 25. What if the horse I buy has more potential than I have talent?

A good trainer will select a horse to suit the rider, even if the rider has ambitions that exceed his skill—unless, of course, the rider has made it clear that he or she will act as a sponsor and purchase a horse for the trainer to ride and show. Trainer Lendon Gray has said: "Many owners have said to me, 'But he is such a wonderful horse, and you will help him realize his potential in a way I cannot.' I tell those owners that the horse doesn't care if he goes to the Olympics; he's just as happy (or even happier) simply helping the owner learn how to ride. It is the owner's horse, he bought it, and he should find enjoyment in his horse in any manner he wishes. Yes, it can be hard for us as trainers to watch a talented horse not be ridden to his potential. But what matters is that horse and rider are happy."

tip 26. Can I use my talented horse to win at lower levels?

Perhaps, but judge Max Gahwyler cautions that "some competitors buy very advanced horses, then drop them down into Training Level, which is obvious to any experienced observer. I consider this practice to be unfair to the other competitors, and one that should not rate very high with judges. . . . But after a while, even these horses regress to the level of their riders. No horse stays better than the rider on his back for very long."

tip 27. Settling in.

Once you have made your choice and the horse is yours, don't rush right into work. Take a week or more and get to know him. Make sure he is relaxed in his new surroundings; give him a chance each day to look around and explore. Ask your veterinarian to perform a preliminary exam to determine the horse's condition, and follow his or her advice in setting up a feeding program that will meet the horse's needs. Ask whether or not the horse needs the services of an equine dentist. Call the farrier and ask him to observe the horse in motion before making any decisions about shoeing. Don't start right off with schooling sessions: take time to hack cross-country (if he has had trail experience, otherwise wait until a rider friend can take you out); take time for the two of you to create a bond. Work on getting him fit by free lungeing, lungeing, working in hand, and riding at the walk and trot. Once you feel comfortable with each other, start with short schooling sessions, focusing on one lesson at a time. Vary the program and gradually increase the amount of time for each session.

Every horse needs time to be a horse, even during intensive training, and daily turnout in a grassy field is a good way to provide it.

Chapter 4

Stable and Equipment

Unless you have a barn in your backyard

with enough space for an arena and a paddock, as well as the time to provide daily care for your horse, chances are that you will want to find a stable where you can board your horse. Not only will this be more convenient for you on days you can't ride, but it can also provide a supportive, friendly atmosphere in which to ride. But not all stables may the right place for you and your horse. Here are some tips for stable selection.

Dressage riders tend to flock together, sharing tips and advice as well as the arena. Horses, too, are herd animals and like to work in the presence of other horses. This atmosphere is also useful preparation for the confusion one often meets at shows. (photo: Kate Rudich)

tip 28. Ride in company.

Many dressage riders prefer to work one-on-one with a trainer and to have the arena to themselves when they are schooling on their own. This can be advantageous for those who have difficulty concentrating. Keep in mind, however, that horses are herd animals and dressage tests are not performed in a vacuum but on show grounds—where there are many other horses, each doing his own thing. In the past, riding masters often worked with groups of students; even today, one can observe group practice at the Spanish Riding School and other equestrian centers. A very important aspect of riding in company is proper behavior. Every ring has its rules, and it behooves the new-comer to learn and observe them. Some rules are universal (for example, keep at least a horse's length between yourself and the rider ahead of you; never pass another horse going in the same direction but circle or cross the arena; do not cross the path of another horse; ride closer to the center at slower gaits, and so on) and some may be specific to the facility where you are riding.

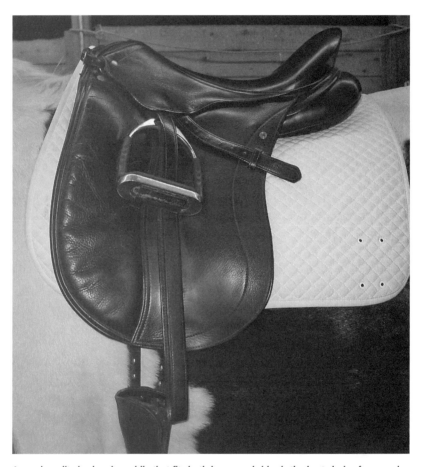

A good-quality broken-in saddle that fits both horse and rider is the best choice for a novice dressage rider. (photo: Carol Epstein)

tip 29. Don't rush to order a new saddle.

One of the most important investments a rider can make after paying for the horse is a saddle that fits both horse and rider. Wait until the horse has been in work, however, before investing in an expensive new or custom-made saddle. Horses continue to grow after the age of five and dressage work will strengthen a horse's back, so what may fit a horse perfectly at first may not be right a year later. In the meantime, use a saddle in which you feel comfortable and secure, so long as it fits the horse, whether it is a well-broken-in used saddle or an inexpensive model. Revisit the situation occasionally to make sure the saddle continues to do its job by enabling the horse to do his.

The nylon strap around Howard's neck below the reins was designed by trainer Wendy Murdoch to help riders like Elizabeth keep (or regain) their balance without pulling back on the reins. (photo: Wendy Murdoch)

tip 30. Use a safety strap.

If your seat is not as secure as you would like, consider placing a stirrup leather around the horse's neck; this will give you something other than the reins to hold onto if you lose your balance and will save your horse's mouth. Some riders recommend a bucking strap, which attaches to the rings in front of the saddle; but the stirrup leather encourages you to reach down the horse's neck rather than pull back, thus developing the proper reflexes for rein use. Trainer Wendy Murdoch has developed the Equistrap, a nylon strap that goes around the base of the horse's neck but is not tied together, so it is easier to hold with the reins and allows the rider to move his or her hands to the side for turning. If you lose your balance, pull upward on the strap (so your hands are about an inch higher than you might normally carry them) and allow your elbows and hips to be soft so that you can pull yourself into the saddle. Once you have established a fixed (but not rigid) hand position using the strap, you will learn to stay upright and ride forward to your hands, instead of pulling back on the reins.

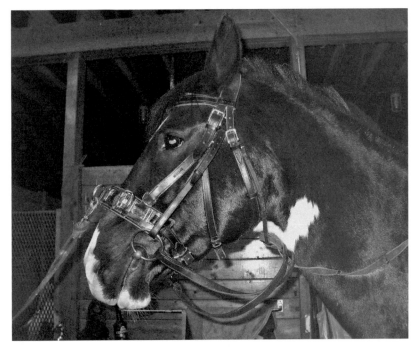

In preparation for lungeing, the reins have been twisted and held up by the cheekstrap. The cavesson, to which the lunge line is attached, is placed over the bridle and held in place with two straps. (photo: Carol Epstein)

tip 31. Keep your training equipment simple.

Although the ultimate goal of the dressage rider is to achieve perfect collection with a double bridle, a mild snaffle is the bit of choice for most horses in training. Trainers often have favorite bits for different levels of training, depending on a horse's particular needs. Dropped or flash nosebands need not be used, except to prevent horses from opening their mouths or putting their tongues over the bit. Ask your trainer for advice. The other important pieces of equipment you will need are a lunge line, a lunge whip, and a cavesson, since you should avoid attaching the lunge line to the bit itself (see tip 42). A surcingle with side reins and overchecks may also be useful for lungeing, but follow the advice of your trainer in using it and other equipment, some of which can be very risky. For example, trainer and judge Cindy Sydnor cautions: "The use of draw reins to force a 'frame' can do tremendous damage to any horse. This is one of the prime sources of distress and overflexion in horses. Draw reins are one of the worst techniques used in the name of shortening the time necessary to train a horse."

tip 32. Look for a barn where other dressage riders keep their horses.

Although your horse may be well taken care of at a hunter-jumper barn, you will likely have difficulty getting access to enough open space in the arena to set up a dressage arena. Also, the other riders may not be willing to let you lunge or free lunge your horse in the arena, which is probably going to be full of jumps. You will want to use cavalletti or poles for schooling, and an occasional gymnastic use of low jumps can provide a nice change of pace for your horse—but it is not easy to perfect flying changes when you are avoiding a rider on a course of fences. A barn that houses a number of dressage horses is also likely to sponsor schooling shows and offer clinics with visiting experts. There may also be a resident trainer or trainers, and other boarders can provide help by videotaping your schooling sessions or noting problems you might be having. It can also be very useful to watch other riders having lessons (providing you have asked for permission to listen in).

Chapter 5

Moving Ahead

A rider who has mastered the basics of equitation and has bought a suitable horse is now in a position to teach the horse. This is most effectively achieved with the assistance of a trainer or coach, one with a great deal of experience with many different horses. Your riding instructor may be that person, but if you are looking for someone with more experience in breaking young horses, for example, you may need to look elsewhere for help.

tip 33. Breaking in a young horse.

If you want to work with a young horse, find a trainer who specializes in the particular breed and has a great deal of experience with break-ins. This trainer can help you select the horse and then give it a good start. Your own involvement may be minimal at first, especially if the trainer does not work in your area, but you should count on a transitional training period when you work alongside the trainer in order to understand what the horse has learned. Bring your riding instructor or coach along so that they too spend some time with the horse and the trainer before "graduation."

tip 34. Upgrading your horse.

If you find that you and your horse have reached a kind of plateau and you do not have access to a trainer on a regular basis, there are a number of ways to move ahead. You may, of course, consult one or more of the excellent books available on the subject (see suggestions in Further Reading). There are also videotapes that provide tips and exercises. The dressage magazines also contain very useful articles every month. But to teach your horse piaffe or passage when you do not have experience with these movements really requires the help of an expert. If you admire the work of a particular trainer, look for clinics to which you might bring your horse. Or ask the horse's original trainer to take the horse back for a refresher course.

Part II

Training

"Ask often, be happy with little, and reward always."

—Captain Etienne Beudant

Chapter 6

Approaches to Training

This section is not intended to teach the

reader how to ride a trained horse or how to train a young horse. Instead, I offer tips and suggestions from the experts on different aspects of training—concepts that are not always explained clearly in the how-to books.

tip 35. Buy a notebook and plan to fill it with your own tips.

It isn't easy taking notes while you are in the saddle, but writing down some of your trainer's advice after you dismount will help you remember it later on. Also write down exercises that your trainer recommends you work on when you are riding on your own. And, of course, take notes while reading books or articles in the dressage magazines; underlining useful tips can be helpful, but you should make a note of the source so that you will be able to find it again.

tip 36. Design a lesson plan before you start.

Before you school your horse, make a plan as to what you would like to accomplish that day. Use your warm-up time to assess the horse's mood and flexibility and then proceed with the schooling session, starting with what he knows and moving on to movements he doesn't know or doesn't perform well. Perhaps you want to correct a faulty bend or an imperfect haunches-in. Perhaps you want to teach a new movement. Perhaps you feel the horse has had enough schooling for several days in a row and needs to get out and see the world. Whatever you decide to work on, don't make it the same program day after day or you run the risk of allowing the horse to become bored or resistant.

Praise is just as important a part of training as discipline and patience, whether it takes the form of a "good boy" or a pat on the neck after a correct movement or a carrot after a good working session. (photo: Mari Austad)

tip 37. Use patience in teaching a new movement.

When you are teaching your horse a new movement, be patient but persistent until he does what you want—or something close to what you want. Then praise him and allow him to walk forward on a loose rein. Come back to the movement again, repeating your aid until he responds. If he doesn't respond correctly or at all, repeat the aid and reinforce it with a slight pressure of the whip. When the horse does respond, praise him again, repeat the movement, and end the lesson so that he has a chance to think about it all night! Include the movement in the next schooling session and make it part of his regular routine.

Whether you live in the city or the country, getting out of the arena for a ride is a wonderful way to clear the mind, both human and equine. (photo: Kate Rudich)

tip 38. Hack out for a change of pace.

One of the great joys of riding a horse is going out on a trail or through a park. Hacking out is also one of the great training aids for people (and horses) who are very serious about their work. At least once a week, change your training routine and give both yourself and your horse a break. If you have no access to a trail, consider trailering to a place where you can hack out, preferably one with a few hills. (The trailer lesson will be valuable in any case.) If you don't know the trails, ask a friend to be your guide. A good strong canter uphill will do wonders for strengthening the hindquarters, and the downhill walking will help the horse find his balance. If you don't have access to trails, just walk up and down the driveway. Don't worry if the horse is not on the bit (under control, yes, but not collected). Relax and have fun. Hacking out will clear the head of both horse and rider and should be considered a regular reward, even if it is only for a few moments after a lesson or instead of a lesson.

tip 39. Learn the art of giving.

We always expect the horse to give us his best effort, but we must remember that this is a two-way street. As you teach the horse to respond to your leg or your seat, and he accepts your cue by bending, relaxing his jaw, and lowering his head, reward him immediately by loosening the reins slightly (but not throwing them away). You may then feel him take up the bit on his own, moving from the inside leg to the outside rein. This give-and-take relationship with your horse is the ultimate goal of dressage. Be lavish with praise when the horse does what he is asked and when he lowers his head toward the ground at the trot or canter, because this means he is using his back rather than pulling with his front end.

Chapter 7

Training Techniques

Because each horse is different from every other horse, the approach to training will vary with the individual, but there are a few basic techniques that are worth mastering, as they have uses at different stages of training.

Working a horse at liberty is a useful form of exercise when one may observe a horse's natural gaits. (photo: Mary Bloom)

tip 40. Use free lungeing as a warm-up.

If you have exclusive access to a relatively small enclosed ring, a nice way to warm the horse up (or get the bucks out) is to free lunge (or loose school) your horse. Hold a lunge whip in your *outside* hand (your right hand if the horse is tracking left) and position your body behind the horse's midsection. From the middle of the ring, direct the horse to move ahead along the rail by pointing the whip toward the hindquarters and using your voice. Keep your body parallel with his haunches; if you move toward the horse's front end, he will probably stop (the correct response) or turn around (which may not be what you want at that moment). If he moves toward you, point the whip toward his shoulder to keep him out on the circle; if he slows down, gently swing the lunge whip up in the air in the direction of movement. The horse should perform his gaits, halts, transitions, and changes of direction at your command, with his inside ear aimed in your direction, indicating that you have his undivided attention.

tip 41. Free lungeing, step two.

If you are using the session as a warm-up before riding, free lunge your horse with saddle and bridle in place. Twist the reins under the horse's neck and secure them with the cheek strap, or put them behind the stirrups, which should also be tied up to prevent flapping. You may also add a lungeing rig (a surcingle with side reins and overchecks), which will help the horse find the right position for his head and neck. Be very cautious with a young horse, however, as tight settings may do more damage than good. Follow your trainer's advice. Reiner Klimke recommends keeping the side reins an even length for free lungeing in order to help the horse remain straight.

tip 42. Learn the art of lungeing.

Almost everyone knows about the value of lungeing a horse, especially during the breaking-in process—teaching the horse to move forward, getting the kinks out before you ride, teaching a horse to bend, and so on. But effective lungeing is not as easy as it looks. Do not just attach the end of the lunge line to the bit. Use the middle ring of a lungeing cavesson; this will save the horse's mouth, and you won't have to change it when you want the horse to go in the other direction. If you don't have a cavesson, you may put the line through the inside ring, run it over the poll or under the chin, and attach it to the outside bit. But a cavesson is the safest device and well worth the investment. Side reins are a substitute for the rider's hands and will help the horse reach for the bit with confidence. The length of the side reins will decrease as training progresses, but the inside rein should be at least two or three holes shorter than the outside.

Lunar is ready for lungeing, with his cavesson and two sets of side reins in place. Note that his trainer has used a surcingle without a saddle. Be sure that the surcingle girth is tight before you begin lungeing, as it may slip during exercise. (photo: Kate Rudich)

Lungeing is an effective training technique, especially for young horses. This mare is fully garbed in her saddle and bridle, plus a cavesson to which the lunge line is attached. She is also wearing a rig in which side reins and overchecks run from the surcingle, which lies over the saddle, to the bridle, which is under the cavesson; this helps the horse adjust the position of her head.

tip 43. Lungeing, part two.

Watch your trainer and other experts lunge their horses and make mental notes of their body language, and their voice and whip signals. Most will place their bodies at the level of the horse's girth with the arm holding the line bent at the elbow and on a line with the horse's head, and the arm holding the whip at a right angle facing the horse's hind end. This position forms a triangle that will enable you to control the horse's movement much as if you were in the saddle. Remember that the whip is a substitute for the legs, while the lunge line and side reins are substitutes for the hands.

Bonus tip: Also known as double lungeing, long lining, or long reining, working a horse from the ground while walking behind holding two long reins can help straighten a horse, if done properly. As with other training techniques, however, follow your trainer's advice, as double lungeing can also cause harm if not employed correctly for the horse's particular needs.

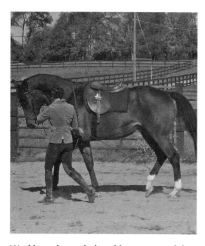

Working a horse in hand is a very useful way of teaching a young horse basic movements, as Tina is doing here with Kashan, moving him first straight ahead and then in a shoulder-in. (photo courtesy Tina Cope)

In-hand work has also been used for centuries to train horses to perform airs above the ground, as in this illustration from the Duke of Newcastle's eighteenth-century manual *A General System of Horsemanship*.

tip 44. Work in hand.

Experienced dressage trainers use work in hand to teach horses advanced movements, such as piaffe, levade, and other airs above the ground. Working a horse in hand also affords the trainer or rider a great opportunity for teaching a horse shoulder-in and other lateral movements, rein back, halt, and other relatively simple movements at a much earlier stage of training. Watch the videotapes produced by Bettina Drummond, a classical dressage trainer who favors Iberian horses (Lusitanos and Andalusians) but works with many other breeds. Her ability to relax a nervous or young horse and to find a harmonious working relationship with virtually any horse is remarkable to watch.

Trainer Tina Cope rides her mare Endless Love over a series of poles set at different heights to keep the horse alert and to help improve her balance and timing. (photo courtesy Tina Cope)

Bonus tip: If you do not have cavalletti, plain poles will work. But be sure they are fixed in place, as horses often ignore them and may cause them to roll, risking an accident.

tip 45. Make use of cavalletti.

Follow the suggestions of the German trainers Ingrid and Reiner Klimke: "Within the field of dressage training, cavalletti are especially beneficial to the basic gaits of the walk and trot. Fixed distances between the single rails serve to improve the time and balance of the movement (action). Simply by having to step higher, both carriage and animation are increased. And from there, it is not very far to the first steps of the passage." If the horse has not been worked with cavalletti, start with one rail at the lowest level and walk with a loose rein. Gradually increase the number, in a straight line just inside the wall of the arena. The distance between poles will depend on the size of the horse and the length of stride. As the horse becomes accustomed to the exercise and you can ride with light contact, the cavalletti may be turned to medium and then maximum height. The next step is to trot over at least three or four cavalletti at the lowest height about 4 feet apart, increasing both height and distance as the horse increases in confidence. Then you may put three or four poles fanned out on a half circle, which is more difficult for the horse.

Chapter 8

The Gaits

Virtually everyone who rides horseback

knows the basic gaits—walk, trot (or jog), canter (or lope), and gallop. One of the most interesting aspects of dressage is that within these gaits are many variations, involving not only collection and extension, but also transitions between gaits, as well as the halt and the rein back.

The medium walk, above, is a very different gait from the free walk, below. Both are very important gaits in any dressage test.

tip 46. Work at the walk.

Never underestimate the usefulness of the walk—or rather, the walks, as there are several variations of the gait: the medium (or working) walk, collected walk, extended walk, free walk, and Spanish walk. French trainer Michel Henriquet believes that "the walk is the most indispensable gait for teaching the aids, the movements, and the exercises. The rapid gaits always bring about a greater nervous tension and cadences that are more delicate to sustain." And in the show ring, according to judge Max Gahwyler, "the walk is also a dead giveaway of the education the horse has received and the level of knowledge and experience of the rider or instructor. . . . But let's not forget that horses generally have correct gaits before they are trained, and they should maintain correct gaits while they are being progressively educated." The medium walk, in which the horse moves forward energetically while the rider keeps a light contact with his mouth, is a crucial element in gymnastic exercises that focus on transitions to and from the trot and canter and in teaching lateral movements and the art of bending (see tip 55).

tip 47. Practice the free walk.

In lower levels of competition, the score for a free walk is multiplied by a coefficient of two, indicating that judges take very seriously a horse's ability to walk forward willingly on a long (not loose) rein, but in a relaxed manner with his head stretched and lowered. In training, the free walk is a useful way to begin a warm-up session to loosen the horse's muscles, to encourage him to reach for the bit, and to move his hind legs underneath himself in order to stay balanced. The lowered head position at the end of a session indicates not that the horse is heavy on the forehand (unless he is pulling down) but that he has stretched his topline and used his back and hindquarters properly during the session. The extended walk required at higher levels is not the same as a free walk but is a gait in which the horse demonstrates the maximum length of his stride while pushing from behind as he seeks contact with the bit. The head is stretched forward but not down. The extended walk is usually taught after the collected walk has been achieved.

tip 48. Use the leg yield to improve the walk.

The German judge Josef Knipp suggests that the rider use leg yielding to "improve the rhythm and activity at the walk, because the rider can influence her horse's hind leg at the right movement more easily. The rider gives the aid when the hind leg is leaving the ground and she feels the horse's response to the leg aid in her seat as the horse steps under the energy flows through the back to a receiving hand." Too strong a hand, he believes, blocks the hind legs so they cannot come forward, thus impairing the rhythm of the walk. The leg yield is used mostly to teach young horses to respond to leg pressure, but it can also be used as a loosening-up exercise before starting the shoulder-in. Most trainers do not use or encourage leg yielding as a horse progresses, as it tends to put a horse on the forehand rather than on the haunches, but FEI* judge Hilda Gurney believes that the leg yield is an essential step in the training process, because it serves as a simple means of introducing the concept of lateral movement.

Fédération Equestre Internationale

Bettina Drummond is sitting to Jabuti's medium trot, above, but she chooses to post to Kiko's trot, below, as he is a young horse just past the break-in period.

tip 49. Work on rhythm and cadence at the trot.

Some trainers will say that the walk is where one really starts training a young horse, but most agree that the place to start is the two-beat trot. As with the walk, there are several categories of trot, but the working trot is the one that will serve as the foundation on which much of the horse's training will be built. The first level of the German training scale—rhythm—can be tested and perfected at the working trot, from which one may work on transitions to halt, walk, and canter; on shoulder-in and other lateral movements; and on extension and collection within the gait. The rising trot frees the horse's back during the moment of suspension, and this encourages forward movement. All dressage riders aspire to the sitting trot, however, for it is with a secure seat and placing one's weight on the haunches that the horse will develop self-carriage, which indicates that the horse has properly engaged his hindquarters. A useful exercise is to practice the transition from rising to sitting trot without any change in cadence or rhythm.

Here Bettina and Jabuti perform a canter on the left lead.

tip 50. Use the canter for balance.

The canter is not just a collected gallop (a four-beat gait) but a three-beat gait of its own, and many trainers recommend that a young horse not be cantered until he has begun to understand collection. The eighteenth-century master François Robichon de la Guérinière wrote: "It is a practiced rule by all of the skilled masters that a horse must not be cantered until he has been suppled at the trot, so that he brings himself forward at the canter without leaning or pulling on the hand."

Trainer Stephen Aust observes that if a horse equates canter with *fast*, it is a difficult habit to correct, and he suggests that the canter be introduced while hacking out rather than during a session in the ring. Cantering uphill will oblige a horse to use his hindquarters, which will help strengthen it for the collected canter you will eventually want to achieve.

A square halt, which every dressage judge wants to see.

tip 51. Come to a halt.

Every horse will stop sooner or later, but it is best if he does so when and where you want, standing square, balanced, and completely still, with his neck flexed and his mind ready for your next command. There should be no moving around, no nodding for rein or raising of the head, no shifting of weight from one leg to another. But this perfect halt does not come easily, especially to a young, spirited, or nervous horse. When you start to teach your horse to halt, don't worry at first about standing square; just keep the horse still for a moment or two and then praise him. Practice this until he gets the idea. Once your horse understands that he is supposed to stand still, you can suggest gently with your legs that he move one or another leg beneath himself to a balanced position. Even better, when you use your aids for the halt, squeeze slightly with your legs to get him to lower his haunches and bring his hind legs underneath. Be sure to praise him with a pat on the neck and a "good boy."

Keep in mind Nuno Oliveira's wise words: "During the course of dressage training, it is often necessary to return frequently to correct halts, especially from the trot. The transition from the halt to the trot, and from the trot to the halt, is one of the keystones of good dressage training, and makes the horse properly collected."

tip 52. Transitions, transitions, transitions.

Transitions are a crucial element in dressage. Judges pay as much attention to transitions as they do to the gaits, because it is during transitions from one gait to the other that the horse's submission to the rider (or lack of it) is most evident. Lateral work, such as the shoulder-in (see tip 57), is one way to achieve submission, and the half halt (tip 53), a longitudinal exercise, is another. Transitions between and within gaits are of the utmost importance in training a horse to achieve self-carriage. As Canadian Olympian Cindy Ishoy puts it, "Transitions are the basis for strengthening the horse's hind end, for softening the neck and jowl area and for total body conditioning, which prepares him for higher-level movements. When ridden correctly from the back of the horse to the front, transitions put the horse back onto his hocks, which strengthens his hind end and makes him more supple throughout his back." She recommends practicing walk-trot transitions on circles and in serpentines as part of the daily routine.

tip 53. Master the half halt.

The point of the half halt is to transfer the horse's energy and weight to his hindquarters in order to make him more balanced and collected. Olympic rider Guenter Seidel offers this advice: "Theoretically, to begin the half halt, you will use your leg and push forward with the seat. Your horse should go to the hand and have a nice connection. . . . The problem is that sometimes the horse doesn't understand and he reacts incorrectly. . . . We simply have to backtrack to basic transitions that build the horse's understanding of the half halt: walk-halt, trot-walk-halt. . . . If your horse understands go, he will go correctly to the hand. If he understands stop, then he will respond to the preparation to stop (or the preparation for a downward transition)—which is a half halt. The half halt is very simple, so keep it simple, and exercise patience in helping your horse to understand what you want."

tip 54. Don't hurry the rein back.

Many novices are surprised that backing a horse up is not one of the first lessons, but in fact the rein back is usually not taught until after the horse has learned a square, balanced halt. The rein back is actually treated like a forward gait, with the seat and legs (slightly behind the girth) asking for impulsion while the hands keep the horse from moving forward, not by pulling but by resisting forward movement. The horse should move backward in a straight line and with a certain degree of animation, as in a forward gait. Ask for only one or two strides at first and never more than four or five strides, unless you are using the rein back as punishment for disobedience.

Chapter 9

Intermediate Work

Although lateral and longitudinal exercises are not often the first movements that a beginning dressage rider is taught, they are so basic that they should be considered an integral part of elementary schooling. Lateral suppling (as in the shoulder-in and half pass) helps make a horse straight, whereas longitudinal suppling (transitions, rein back) makes the back more flexible and enables the horse to engage his hindquarters.

Bettina is using her inside leg and seat bone here to bend Jabuti to the left, while her outside leg rests slightly behind the girth to prevent his hindquarters from swinging out.

tip 55. Use your legs and seat to bend the horse.

Lateral flexion is the key to the circle, the shoulder-in, and just about everything else in dressage. Instead of using your inside rein to get your horse to flex to the left or right as you round a corner or make a circle, use your inside leg as a post around which the horse turns (weight down in the stirrup, which remains at the girth), your inside seat bone positioned ahead of the outside seat bone, your outside rein as regulator of both speed and degree of flexion, and your outside leg slightly behind the girth to keep the haunches from moving outward. The most important thing to remember is not to apply pressure on the inside rein to pull the horse's neck around. In fact, you shouldn't be using the inside rein at all, except perhaps to keep the horse's head low and relaxed (see tip 62). Indeed, when you feel like using the inside rein, use the inside leg and seat bone instead.

tip 56. Work in circles (not ovals).

Riding a perfect circle takes precision and practice. Measure a 20-meter circle (65.61 feet in diameter) by drawing or scratching a line in the surface of your ring. Then place a cone at each quarter mark just inside the circle. As you perform the circle—at the walk, trot, or canter—think of it as broken into four equal parts, and concentrate on making each quarter the same rather than focusing on the whole circle. (Be sure to keep your inside leg at the girth as the pole around which your horse is bending, and put your outside leg slightly behind the girth to keep the haunches from drifting out.) When you feel good about the circle at the walk, try the trot and then the canter. If you feel your horse is supple enough, move on to increasingly smaller circles (15 and 10 meters).

Trainer Charles de Kunffy suggests that the rider not visually search for the pattern of the circle in the sand but ". . .'feel' the circle when a well-bent horse in good balance and impulsion simply returns to the point of his origins without any 'steering efforts' at all!"

Bonus tip: For perfecting the circle, Australian trainer Eleanor Russell suggests that you place 5-gallon drums about 2 feet apart on each side of the line at different points of the circle and ride between them. You can make a game of it by penalizing yourself a dollar (or putting it in the custom-made saddle fund) for each time your horse touches a drum.

Bonus tip: A valuable exercise is to make squares as well as circles, using the corner of the arena at first but eventually working on squares in the middle of the arena. You will be expected to square your corners in your dressage tests, so why not start perfecting them now! Prepare for each corner a stride ahead of time, and as you turn, ask the horse to pivot and then move forward briskly toward the next corner. As the horse becomes accustomed to the exercise, you can turn the corner more smoothly.

Tina Cope is performing a left shoulder-in on her horse Jesse, moving to the right but bent to the left. (photo courtesy Tina Cope)

Bonus tip: Aside from the training benefits to be gained from learning the correct shoulder-in, the rider of a spooky horse will find it a useful tactic to keep the horse's attention away from some suspicious object that might elicit a reaction.

tip 57. Master the shoulder-in.

Bending on the circle is the most effective way to start learning the shoulder-in. As the horse comes back to the wall, move him along the wall instead of following the circle, keeping him bent around your inside leg as you move away from the direction he is facing. The horse's inside foreleg crosses in front of the outside foreleg and his inside hind crosses in front of the outside hind leg. (The term *shoulder-in*, incidentally, does not refer to the shoulders' position relative to the wall of the arena but to the position of the inside shoulder.) A left shoulder-in indicates that the horse is bent around to the left (although he is in fact moving to the right). The seventeenth-century master François Robichon de la Guérinière, who invented the shoulder-in, believed it was the "first and last lesson you give your horse," the one that teaches him to respond to your inside leg and to bring his inside hind leg under his body. As Nuno Oliveira put it: "The shoulder-in is the aspirin of equitation; it cures everything."

Lunar is concentrating hard on his haunches-in, bending and moving to his right by crossing his left legs over his right legs, front and back. (photo: Kate Rudich)

tip 58. Explore the other lateral movements.

In the shoulder-in, the angle of the horse's shoulders to the track is about 30 degrees; the shoulder-fore has less of an angle and is a useful preparatory exercise for the shoulder-in. The reverse (or counter) shoulder-in (or shoulder-out) is the same as the shoulder-in, except that the horse's shoulders are closer to the wall than the hindquarters. Like the shoulder-in, this lateral movement strengthens the muscles of the inside hip and hock. Haunches-in (or *travers*) is a three-track exercise in which the horse looks in the direction he is moving. Haunches-out (or *renvers*) is the same as haunches-in, except that the hindquarters are closer to the wall than the shoulders. These are useful exercises to learn before starting the half-pass and canter depart, and they strengthen the stifle muscles of the outside hind leg.

The aids for the half-pass are like those for haunches in, but the horse is moving forward and with less bend, his front end slightly ahead of his hindquarters.

tip 59. Move on the diagonal: the half-pass.

In the half-pass, the most difficult lateral movement, the horse moves diagonally to one side or the other, bending in the direction of the movement while remaining parallel to the wall, with front and back outside legs crossing over in front of the inside legs. (By contrast, in the leg yield, the horse moves forward for one stride and to the side for another, remaining straight rather than bent around the inside leg.) The half-pass is usually performed from one corner to the other on a diagonal line, or from the centerline to the wall. The movement is similar to the haunches-in (or haunches-out) except that the horse moves mostly forward and somewhat sideways in the direction that he faces, with his forehand slightly ahead of his haunches.

tip 60. Work on longitudinal exercises.

Just as lateral exercises improve flexibility of the hind legs, longitudinal exercises increase flexibility of the horse's back by lengthening and shortening his stride at all three gaits, as well as at the halt and rein back. Start by lengthening the stride of the walk down the long side of the arena by applying leg pressure and resisting slightly with your hands to keep him from moving ahead too quickly or falling on his forehand. Shorten or collect the stride at the end of the arena by resisting with your hands while keeping your legs in contact with his sides. Vary the exercise by lengthening on the short side and shortening on the long side, so that the horse does not learn to anticipate the exercise. Do the same exercise at the trot and the canter. Eventually, when you have achieved true collection, you will be able to perform true extended gaits.

tip 61. Work on a series of exercises at each schooling session.

Each lesson plan should consist of a set of figures, never performed in exactly the same order but always equally in each direction: squares (with pivots at each corner), circles of different sizes (from a 20-meter circle to the 6-meter volte), serpentines (a series of loops down the length of the ring), frequent changes of rein (or direction), figure eights, and spirals on the circle. These exercises may be done at the walk, trot, or canter, preferably all three. Intersperse these figures with lateral work, such as the shoulder-in down one side of the arena, alternating with straight movement along the rail. If your horse bends more easily to one side than the other (as most horses do), you might start in that direction first and then change rein. And don't forget to allow the horse the opportunity every so often to stretch and relax on a loosened rein.

Here Tina rewards Jesse for responding to her aids by giving with the inside rein. (photo courtesy Tina Cope)

tip 62. Don't overuse the inside rein.

One of the most common problems in virtually every novice dressage rider is overuse of the inside rein. Pulling back on the inside rein when you are trying to bend your horse will simply make it more difficult for him to move forward and keep the inside hind leg from coming underneath—exactly the opposite of what you want. The inside rein needs to be low and steady but giving, so that the horse controls the inside half of the bit. The horse seeks contact with the outside rein, but the pressure on the inside rein should be only as heavy as the weight of the rein itself. An exception to this would be in training a very young horse to bend by using a direct or opening rein, but this is a temporary measure to be discontinued as soon as the horse learns to move into the outside rein from the inside leg. Trainer Eleanor Russell calls the outside rein the rider's guardian angel. Think of it as your brake (controlling the forward movement), your steering wheel (to keep the horse's shoulders from drifting or falling out of the circle), and the main point of contact with your horse's mouth when bending.

tip 63. Use your aids with subtlety.

Nuno Oliveira wrote: "The schooling of the horse consists of a consecutive series of exercises in which, being sure of geometrical precision, the horse is placed in the right position to execute them. He must be placed correctly and left alone so that he can succeed. Once he is properly positioned, it is not desirable to continue giving the aids which direct the exercise, but merely to use those necessary to intervene in controlling the action."

Instructor David Collins puts it this way: "As with many concepts in riding, the principles at the beginning and advanced levels are basically the same; they just become more refined as one progresses. Riding a horse becomes more like conducting an orchestra. Each instrument must be played individually before they can be played together in concert. When the result is correct, the rider only applies an aid when he wants to change something, and the rider remembers that the most important part of applying an aid is the release. When all of this functions according to plan, the rider plays the horse between the aids. The result is a happy, rhythmic horse."

tip 64. Learn the five rein effects.

Practice these classic rein aids, which involve the use of an active hand working with a passive hand that keeps contact but does not interfere with the action. As Jean Froissard tells us, the first two reins affect the forehand: the opening (or direct) rein is used to turn the horse by moving the horse's nose in the direction you wish to go, and the indirect (or neck) rein, in which one lays the rein against the neck, is used to move the horse in the direction of movement. The other three reins affect the hindquarters: the direct rein of opposition (in which the inside rein moves back parallel to the horse's body and causes the hindquarters to move to the outside); the indirect rein of opposition in front of the withers (which makes the horse pivot away from the active rein, with his shoulders moving away from the rein, the haunches going toward it); and the indirect rein of opposition behind the withers (which causes the horse to move obliquely away from the rein with shoulders and haunches moving in the same direction).

The counter-canter is essentially a canter on the wrong lead; it is also a basic step in teaching a horse flying changes. Here Jesse canters on the right lead going counterclockwise around the ring. (photo courtesy Tina Cope)

tip 65. **Work on the counter-canter.**

This exercise is basically cantering on the wrong lead, but it has an important role in developing a horse's sensitivity to your aids, improving his balance, strengthening his back, and preparing him for flying changes of lead. The aids are the same as those used for the canter except that the *inside* hand and leg are actually *outside*, or closer to the wall. Start teaching the counter-canter by riding a loop down the long side of the arena and heading away from the wall to X (the center of the arena) after the first corner and back to the wall after X. This will keep you from overbending the horse or attempting turns that are sharp enough to encourage the horse to change his lead. Teach your horse to counter-canter before doing flying changes, or he may change leads when you want to stay on the "wrong" lead. If he does change or becomes disunited (with the forelegs on one lead and the hindlegs on the other), don't reprimand him but simply start over and keep him as straight as possible on a very wide turn.

tip 66. Don't obsess about being on the bit.

On the bit is one of the most overused phrases in dressage, especially among novices who worry continually that their horses are not on the bit. A better phrase is *on the aids*, since the bit is not the only factor in the effect that the rider wants to create, which is a working relationship with the horse achieved by seat, legs, and upper body, not just the hand-to-mouth connection. What the rider actually wants is for the horse to *round up*, flex his neck at the poll, and give in to the rider's wishes. This is not something that can be created by side reins or draw reins that force the horse to carry his head in an acceptable position. It is a matter of give and take, of the gradual submission of the horse to the rider's will, not because he must but because he is willing to participate in the activity.

Chapter 10

Advanced Work

The tips in this section are more descrip-

tive than practical, because the movements are performed by relatively advanced riders. Although collected gaits are required for
Second Level tests, extended gaits and flying changes of lead at the
canter are not required until Third Level.

This handsome Lusitano stallion gives Bettina a beautiful collected trot, engaging his hindquarters in pushing from behind.

tip 67. Collection.

In this ultimate step in the German training scale (see tip 6), the hind legs flex more and step farther underneath the horse in the direction of the center of gravity, which lowers the haunches and lightens the forehand so that the horse feels more uphill. The horse's steps in each gait are shorter but the horse does not lose impulsion or energy, and the result is both expressive and elegant. Every horse will benefit from some degree of collection, also called *engagement*, because it encourages balance and self-carriage. It is at this stage that the rider's hands need not move, while the fingers take on "a whispering nature," as Sylvia Loch puts it. "Clearly, in collection, we give with our hands rather less than in extension, but, in general, it is the horse who makes himself light on the rein, by lowering the croup and gathering up through the centre."

The suspension and power of this extended trot would not have been possible without intensive schooling in collection first. (photo: Brenda V. Cataldo, Moments In Time)

tip 68. Extended gaits.

Nothing brings an audience to attention faster than a brilliant extended trot performed by a talented warmblood, but this brilliance is
not easy to achieve (nor sit to). As Nuno Oliveira wrote: "The true
extended trot is the one which is the result of maximum impulsion
in collection. . . . The so-called extended trot, in which the horse stiff-
ens his back, gesticulating with his lower front legs as if 'shooting his
cuffs,' pulling on the reins below a rider who uses his legs at every
stride, cannot be considered as being in the domain of impulsive,
classical equitation." As he explains it, "Any extension should not be
achieved through the reins' force but rather by lowering and empow-
ering the haunches. This is what the French called *The Ramener*, putting the horse gently on the bit to correspond with the degree and
length of pace."

This perfectly collected canter is full of animation and impulsion.

The same energy produces an extended canter diagonally across the arena.

tip 69. The flying change.

First of all, think of the flying change as striking off in the canter, but from the canter rather than from the halt or walk or trot. If your horse can do a consistently smooth canter depart and maintain a collected canter, both on the correct lead and in the counter-canter, then the two of you should not find flying changes very difficult. The critical moment is that you apply your aids just before the horse's legs are all off the ground, so that he will be able to change leads easily. The canter is a three-beat gait, so give the aid after the third beat during that brief, flat moment of suspension.

tip 70. Tempi changes.

Tempi changes offer some of the most fabulous moments in a high-level dressage test, but there is no need to be intimidated by the thought of performing these yourself. Start a series of flying changes down the long side of the arena and try to stay as straight as possible; the wall will help keep the haunches from swinging out. Ask for the flying change every four or five strides—and keep counting "one, two, three, aid" as you go. If the horse becomes excited or anticipates the change, work on something else until he is calm and relaxed.

tip 71. Don't forget the basics.

Olympic rider Guenter Seidel cautions riders not to push their horses too far but to go back to the "basic understanding of the rhythm and the connection even in a high degree of collection. The basics are the biggest part of your daily training even with a Grand Prix horse. As you watch the most successful riders . . . they are doing simple things to improve the connection. You very seldom see them drilling a movement such as half pass or pirouette. . . . I've had my own best tests when I've been working on basic principles that improve my horse's elastic connection, his mental understanding and confidence. Then the work is easy, and that's exactly the goal in my mind."

The canter pirouette, which is difficult to perform correctly, is a good test of a horse's strength and balance.

tip 72. Pirouette.

In watching a horse perform a pirouette at the canter, one can easily see how this movement would have been very useful on the battle-field. You can think of the pirouette as a half-pass on a tiny circle, requiring the highest level of collection. The horse's shoulders rotate around the inside hind leg as he makes a 360-degree turn in place, either at the walk or at the canter (basically a turn on the haunches). The reverse pirouette is in the opposite direction with the horse moving his haunches around his shoulders (a turn on the forehand). The half-pirouette is a 180-degree turn, usually performed at the walk. These very difficult movements require a horse to be balanced, supple, and on the aids.

This young thoroughbred, Fidelio, performs an animated and elegant piaffe. (photo: Carlotta Schaller)

tip 73. Passage and piaffe.

Like tempi changes, these airs above the ground are among the few movements inherited from the classical dressage of the seventeenth century that are still used in competitive dressage today. When performed correctly, they demonstrate a horse's ability to collect, to engage the haunches while maintaining lightness in front. The *passage* can be described as a trot with an extended period of suspension, and *piaffe* can be described as a passage in place. But words alone do not do justice to these elegant movements. Although competitors are not expected to perform either movement until FEI Intermediaire Level, many lower level horses may use piaffe in training in order to help the horse develop self-carriage.

Part III

Showing

"Dressage competition should be some fun, particularly in the lower levels. You are perfectly entitled to smile at the mishaps of your competitors if you can just as easily laugh at yourself and your own misfortunes. Put in perspective, all you have to do is induce your horse to show his best side for five minutes in front of the judge."

—Max Gahwyler, *The Competitive Edge*

Chapter 11

Preparing for the Show

Some dressage riders are competitive

by nature, but even those who are not will occasionally feel the need to gauge their progress by riding a test for a professional judge. Unlike riders in equitation classes, competitors in dressage competitions ride alone in the arena, following specific instructions in tests that are designed to show what a horse is capable of at different levels of training, from Introductory (walk and trot) to FEI Grand Prix, with many levels in between. Judges award the horse points from 1 to 10 for each movement in the test, as well as for general aspects of the performance, and often provide commentary; the total score is given in both numbers and as a percentage.

tip 74. Become a joiner.

If you have never shown your horse, there are a few basic steps to take. First is to join a local dressage association that sponsors shows, either schooling shows (which you will want to start in) or shows that are recognized by the United States Dressage Federation (USDF) and the U.S. Equestrian Federation (USEF), which regulates horse shows of all types throughout the United States. It is a good idea and not very costly to obtain a lifetime membership for your horse in both organizations and to obtain an annual membership in each for yourself. The USEF rule book contains all the regulations (including the dress code) governing dressage competitions (available online at www.usef.org) and the USDF directory contains guidelines, current dressage tests, and just about everything else you will want to know. Your local organization will be the source not only of supportive colleagues but also of calendars listing horse shows that might appeal to you.

tip 75. Volunteer at a dressage competition.

Before you actually enter a competition, take the time to volunteer at a show where you can watch everything that goes on, from the lowest-level tests to Grand Prix and musical freestyle. Call the manager of the show weeks ahead of time and offer your services as a gate-keeper or steward. Eventually you might want to work as a judge's scribe, which will enable you to hear the judge comment on each movement of every ride. Scribing is hard work and demands concentration, but you can learn an incredible amount about what judges look for in evaluating a test.

A schooling show is a fine place to start a career in the dressage arena; dress can be casual and the experience a valuable one.

tip 76. Take advantage of schooling shows.

These events are like dress rehearsals in that one performs a test before a judge in a regulation arena but without the stress of a tough audience. Since schooling shows are not recognized (meaning that your scores will not be on any permanent record or qualify you for awards), most do not require regulation dress, but for reasons given below (see tip 86), it's a good idea to adopt the "dress rehearsal" approach and pretend it is the real thing. The ribbons are real enough, and a good score is something to be proud of. There may be tents, an audience, and other scary things to contend with, but your horse should be prepared for this and made to understand that these are not going to hurt him.

Most schooling show judges are willing to discuss the horse's performance with the rider afterward, offering suggestions about future training. After your test, thank the judge and ask for any advice or tips. You will not be able to do this at a regulation show, but here you can make up for the fact that your scores won't count officially by treating the schooling show as a kind of inexpensive clinic.

tip 77. Select the test.

Your trainer or coach is likely to be the best source of advice as to what test or tests to select. First you must determine the level at which you want to compete. The tests are designed to reflect the horse's gradual progress from one level to the next. The Introductory Level doesn't include a canter, for example. Training Level is a walk-trot-canter test with simple 20-meter circles. First Level introduces lengthening of strides and canter departs at a specific point. And by Third Level, you should be able to achieve both collection and extension at all three gaits, and so on.

If you are a novice, it is usually best to pick a test that is well within the abilities of yourself and your horse. In fact, you may want to select two tests. Not only will the experience be valuable and your chances at a ribbon greater, but you will also be able to erase the experience of a poor test, should you have one, by one that is more satisfying. Judge Janet Hannon recommends that "to be competitive at a fully recognized show, you need to be schooling at a level above where you are showing. . . . A schooling show is the place to stretch yourself."

Bonus tip: It isn't enough to show up on the day of the show and expect to ride a test. You will have to register in advance, because the show officials must determine starting times for each rider. It is usually wise to register considerably ahead of the deadline given by the officials, because many shows attract a large number of competitors, especially at the lower levels.

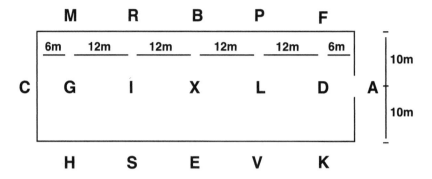

Set up the letters in an arena at home so that you can practice your tests and the horse can get used to their presence. There are two regulation arenas, large (20m x 60m, above) and small (20m x 40m, below).

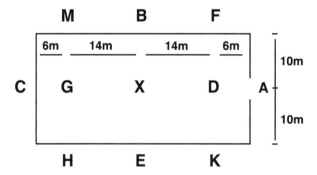

tip 78. Learn your letters.

Before you can start practicing a test, you will, of course, have to educate yourself about the official dressage arena. There are two regulation sizes: the small arena, which is 20 meters wide and 40 meters long (65.61 by 131.2 feet), and the large arena, which is 20 meters wide by 60 meters long (65.61 by 196.85 feet). The next step is to learn the letters and their exact location in the arena. The most important letters for the lower levels are A (where you enter), C (where the judge sits), X (the center of the arena), with E at the middle of the left side (as you face C) and B at the middle of the right. F, M, H, and K are the letters along the rail between C, B, C, and E; D and C are along the centerline. Don't look for any clever mnemonic device to learn the letters. Buy a set of letters and use them at home, or paint them on your walls. Your horse should not meet them for the first time at the show!

tip 79. Learn the test.

Although riders are allowed to have someone (a friend or coach) call the test as they perform it, it is always a good idea to know the test thoroughly before going into the arena before a judge. Write out a copy of the test by hand (this helps get it into the brain). Next, make some copies of the layout of a dressage ring, with letters in their proper places, and draw the test in pencil several times until you feel you know it. Max Gahwyler (whose three-volume work *The Competitive Edge* is an invaluable addition to the dressage rider's library) draws each gait in a different color and uses different symbols for halt, rein back, or whatever else is required in the test. Some riders rely on clever little spiral-bound packages called *Whinny Widgets,* which provide copies of each test in a different level (both written and drawn) that one can carry on horseback during practice.

tip 80. Learn the rules.

Before you enter any competition, consult the U.S. Equestrian Federation rule book (available online at www.usef.org) for all rules that apply to dressage competitions. For example, dressage whips must be no longer than 43.3 inches (including lash). Up to Fourth Level, the dress code calls for a short jacket in a conservative color with a tie, choker or stock tie, breeches or jodhpurs, boots or jodhpur boots, a hunt cap or riding cap with a hard shell, a derby or top hat. Tests above Fourth Level call for a "dark tail coat with top hat, or a dark jacket with a bowler hat or hunt cap, and white or light-colored breeches, stock or tie, gloves and black riding boots." And so on.

tip 81. Practice the test.

It is a good idea to practice the test or tests several times before the show. But don't overdo it or your horse will lose interest, along with the impulsion and energy that judges look for. Instead, practice elements of each test in a different sequence so that you can perfect the canter depart, for example, but not always in the same place. Also try practicing tests that are a bit beyond your horse's ability and training. This will make the competitive test seem easy.

tip 82. Work on your geometry.

The first sight the judge will have of you and your horse is as you trot down the centerline, and the first mark will indicate whether or not your line is straight. Circles must be round, corners must be square, lines must be ridden straight, and so on. An average horse-and-rider team that has a perfect command of their geometry will often score better than a flashy pair that rounds corners, makes egg-shaped ovals instead of circles, and trots in wavy rather than straight lines.

It is a good idea to let your horse have an opportunity to get used to the sight of someone sitting in a trailer or a judge's box before he meets the real thing at the show.

tip 83. School away from home.

Some riders concentrate so hard on perfecting the movements of each test at home that they forget about their horse's state of mind when confronted with a new situation. Not only has the horse been taken by trailer to a strange place, but that strange place is full of other horses not necessarily behaving themselves.

At least once or twice before the actual date of the show, trailer your horse to another facility (after obtaining permission, of course), tack him up in or next to the trailer, and work him for half an hour or more in the ring where other horses are also working, as in a warm-up area. Ask some of the other riders to ride in front of you deliberately or to start cantering behind you, in order to test your horse's reactions (trust me, this will happen in the warm-up area at the show). Keep working your horse and try to keep him focused. Talk to him, but don't say soothing things like "It's okay," as the horse will assume that something is *not* okay. If the horse remains relaxed, one away school may be sufficient. Remember, though, that on the day of the show, you won't be so relaxed, so take that into account in preparing your horse.

You may also try to replicate the dressage arena itself by having a "judge" sit in a chair (or better yet in a trailer) at one end of the ring, blowing a whistle from time to time, standing up and saluting, rustling papers, and otherwise acting like a judge.

tip 84. Watch and learn.

Unless there are very few competitors at your show, it is likely that you and your horse will have some downtime between tests. If so, make a point of watching other riders and making mental notes of their strengths and weaknesses. It is always a treat to watch wonderful riders at the higher levels, but it may be more useful to watch a couple of riders at your own level, especially if they are more experienced than you are. Ask your trainer to point out which riders would be worth watching (even if you are warming up)—not to feel discouraged, but to see how they handle certain aspects of the test.

tip 85. Practice warming up.

The period of time before you actually enter the dressage arena is probably the most crucial few minutes of the entire show. It is often during those few minutes that success is assured, or not. A few days before you go to the show, check your watch before you start to school your horse, and when you feel he is ready to do real work, check your watch again. This will give you some idea how much time you will need before your test to get your horse into a limber, energetic frame.

tip 86. The dress test.

Those who are new to the show ring will undoubtedly want to invest in a nice new pair of boots or an elegant riding coat for the occasion. But don't wait until the day of the show to put them on. Wear them during at least a couple of schooling sessions before the show in order to get used to the new apparel. Nothing is more distracting when you are already nervous than a stiff pair of boots or a formal coat and stock tie. Needless to say, if you are saving some elegant piece of tack for the show, be sure not to introduce it that day, but work with it ahead of time to make sure the horse is comfortable with it.

tip 87. Prepare a show kit.

There are a few items beyond the horse, his tack, and your clothing that you will need to bring to the show grounds. You may not need all of the equipment listed below, but it is always wise to be prepared. Pack up this stuff at least a day before the show so you won't have to worry about it while you are trying to get your horse on the trailer.

Prepare two large waterproof containers, one for horse things (grooming tools, braiding kit, soap, towels, scraper, fly spray, hoof pick, hoof dressing, medical first aid kit, bandages and wraps, extra halter, lead lines, lunge line, etc.) and one for rider things (hat, gloves, hairnet, stock tie and pin, boot-cleaning equipment, extra pair of breeches, clothing brush, raingear, etc.). Include at least two dressage whips of the regulation length (no more than 43.3 inches, including the lash).

Also include at least three buckets (one for last-minute grooming tools and two for the horse), water (if none will be available on-site), hay, and any other feed, supplements, and treats you may need. If you are spending the night, take three times as much hay as you would normally use.

tip 88. Get your paperwork in order.

In a folder, put your horse's recent Coggins test, insurance card, USDF and USEF registration numbers for horse and rider, a copy of the time sheet for entries, and your entry blank. Also include a couple of copies of the tests that you will be performing. Prepare a separate sheet with your horse's name, your name and contact information, and the name of your vet and farrier. Also bring the USDF and USEF rule books.

Your appearance and your performance are what count at a dressage show, and your team will make sure that you get there in one piece! Here the rider listens to last-minute advice from her trainer as a friend stands ready to help with a last-minute crisis.

tip 89. Bring help.

Ask a friend to come along, in addition to your trainer or coach (who may have other riders to worry about). A friend is always a great source of moral support, as well as a loyal servant who will help carry your stuff from the trailer, pick up the official documents, keep track of time, and clap enthusiastically after you finish your test. If the day is hot, ask your friend to carry your jacket while you warm up, to hold your horse as you put it on, and to give your boots a last-minute wipe before your test. Your horse may also need a quick brushing or mouth wipe or some fly spray. While you warm up, your friend should keep an eye on you and carry a bucket filled with towels, fly spray, a brush, water (for you to drink), and anything else you think you might need.

tip 90. Check out facilities at the show.

When you register for the show, find out what will be available (hay, water, stalls for the horses) and make any special requests early. Consider renting a stall for the day, even if the horse is not spending the night. If your tests are spaced out over a day, a comfortable stall out of the sun will give your horse the chance to chill out, especially on a hot day. If you do rent a stall, bring a tool kit with basic equipment, such as a hammer, staple gun, nails, extra rope, snaps, and a drill. Some temporary stalls are sadly lacking in basic amenities (even doors!) and you may have to do some elementary carpentry to make it habitable.

tip 91. Record your performance for posterity.

Arrange in advance to have a friend or a professional photographer to videotape or photograph your tests. Even if you don't do as well as you had hoped, you can always learn a lot from a videotape, and if you do well, the photographs can be sent to all your friends and incorporated into your holiday card for the year!

Chapter 12

Show Day

Up to now, you and your horse have

worked hard, practicing movements and preparing for the dressage test that will accurately demonstrate your achievements. When the moment for your test finally arrives, however, try to forget all those hours of practice and preparation and think about the positive image you are about to present to the judge. As trainer and judge Charles de Kunffy puts it, "Dressage tests must be performed in their totality, not in bits and pieces or as patchwork. Riders should perform each test as an organic whole, like a concert pianist, who does not play notes or measures, but rather the whole musical composition that is beautiful only in its entirety."

tip 92. Be on time.

Even if you have packed everything up and braided your horse (who has never been difficult to load in a trailer), allow at least an extra hour on the day of the show. You might get lost on the way; there might be a lot of traffic. When you get to the show grounds, unload the horse and walk him around to loosen up his muscles and get him used to the place. Once he is comfortable, unload your equipment and begin to think about getting the two of you into battle gear. If he does not settle down, take a few minutes to lunge him, but be sure to ask the show officials where lungeing is allowed.

Ask your friend to pick up your envelope (with start times and number) and review it to make sure everything is correct. Keep your start time in your head, and check before you mount up whether or not the tests are running on schedule. You may be asked to ride ahead of schedule if there have been scratches, although you are not required to do so. If the tests are running late, however, you will have to wait, and this is where the warm-up period can run on far too long for your horse. Keep your horse's confidence level high by asking him to warm up with movements that are on the test, not more difficult, higher-level movements.

tip 93. Warming up, part one.

Once you have figured out where your dressage test will take place (there is often more than one arena), get your horse tacked up and walk him to the warm-up area. Sometimes this is a ring, sometimes an open field. Whichever it is, it is likely to be full of horses going in all different directions, so stay alert and keep your horse focused as you did in the practice sessions. You will probably be a bit nervous and the horse may be distracted by the activity around him as well as by your tension level, so the warm-up may take longer than the time you allotted based on your practice sessions at home. Before your horse has a chance to react to horses coming behind or at him, keep him in a trot and be aware of any fluctuations in tempo caused by the presence of other horses. Don't overdo the actual warm-up, however. Thirty minutes should be enough time to warm up before your test; anything more than that might result in a horse that is either tired or sour.

Just before your test, take advantage of the warm-up area just outside the arena to get your horse accustomed to the footing and try to stay as relaxed as possible while you wait your turn.

tip 94. Warming up, part two.

Just before your test, you will enter an area near the ring itself, which will have the same footing as you will find in the ring (often quite different from the warm-up area). Here you should remain as relaxed as possible and ask the horse to move forward at all gaits and to perform smooth transitions so that he will be familiar with the new footing. Your main job here is to keep the horse at his peak and to listen for the bell or whistle (be sure you know which one your judge is using), which means that you have no more than 90 seconds to enter the ring at A.

At Training Level, the judge does not expect collected or extended gaits, but transitions and figures should be performed willingly and with accuracy. Koda's swishing tail indicates that the horse is resisting Harold's legs. (photos: Patricia Kuehner)

It is at Second Level that dressage really begins, with collected gaits, engagement, impulsion, and acceptance of the bit. (photo courtesy Tina Cope)

tip 95. Focus, focus, focus.

As soon as you trot into the ring at A, breathe regularly, smile, and concentrate on doing what you know you and your horse can do perfectly well. Make your circles round and your corners square, and be sure your transitions occur exactly where they are supposed to occur. If your horse breaks from a canter to a trot or otherwise disobeys, remain calm and just make sure that he obeys the next command. The more focused you are, the more focused the horse is likely to be. Reassure yourself that a bad mark on one movement need not seriously affect your score if the rest of your test is performed well. By all means, judge Linda Zang suggests, show the judge that you are feeling confident and positive and that you believe yours is the best horse ever.

tip 96. Listen to your reader.

If you have someone calling the test for you, make sure that he or she reads only the directions given in the rule book. Anything else, or anything repeated, may result in an error penalty. The caller should stand at B or E, halfway down the arena on one side or the other. Ask your caller ahead of time to give the direction for a particular movement about two letters before the letter where the movement is to take place. In other words, if you are supposed to start a circle to the right at E, have the direction read to you as you pass K (see diagram of large arena on page 138). Riders may have callers at all levels except in final or championship events or in FEI and freestyle tests.

tip 97. Ride straight at the judge.

Trainer Charles de Kunffy offers a useful tip for those first few moments in the ring. Make eye contact with the judge, since eye contact while riding on the centerline is essential to riding a straight track, the first movement on which you will be judged. He also recommends that women bend only their heads at the salute, not their upper bodies, as this runs the risk of upsetting the horse's balance and may even cause him to step back.

Bonus tip: During a dressage test, the rider must not speak or cluck to the horse in any way. Doing so may result in a deduction of two points from the movement you are performing. This sounds easy, but chances are that you often speak to your horse during schooling sessions, either to admonish or to praise, and this may be a difficult habit to break. There is no rule against giving your horse a warm pat on the neck in gratitude after your final salute to the judge, however!

tip 98. Learning after the fact.

Once the test is over and you have thanked the judge for his or her service, leave the ring promptly in a free walk, take care of your horse's needs (which will vary depending on whether or not you have another test to perform), and then take a deep breath and relax as you await your scores, which the judge will submit when all riders in the class have finished their tests. If you are disappointed with your scores, don't crumple up the score card and throw it away. Remember that the judge sees you and your horse perform for only a few moments in a situation of considerable stress. Make a note of the movements in which you had low scores and try to figure out what went wrong. If your horse seemed to overreact in excitement to the pressure (and your stress level), take care to cool him down properly and think about how to deal with this issue in your next schooling session. Instead of focusing on your mistakes, work on the form of your transitions in order to improve balance, as insufficient preparation may have led to imbalance, making mistakes inevitable. Compare the show video of your test with a test made of you taking the same test at home, and ask your trainer to compare them.

tip 99. Understanding the marks.

According to the USEF Rule Book, 0 means not executed; 1 very bad; 2 bad; 3 fairly bad; 4 insufficient; 5 sufficient; 6 satisfactory; 7 fairly good; 8 good; 9 very good; 10 excellent. If you have watched Olympic riders perform, you know that 9s and 10s are rarely given, even to competitors on the highest levels. A 60 percent mark may be a D in school but it is a commendable effort in dressage. Most scores should come somewhere between 5 and 8, which always leaves room for improvement, often suggested by the judges' comments on your card. There are usually several aspects to each mark (straightness, impulsion, contact, obedience, etc.) and the judge must arrive at each mark in a very short period of time, so these comments are rarely very long, but they are meant to be encouraging and helpful and they should be understood as such.

Max Gahwyler writes: "If you are serious about improving, make a chart of the basic movements in your tests and enter the scores from each show. The results may be startling but, on close examination, it will be a valuable indication of what needs to be worked on."

tip 100. Don't get discouraged.

Unless you are terminally competitive (in which case you are probably not reading this book), don't let yourself be discouraged by poor test results or by the length of time it takes for you and your horse to progress to a higher level. Nuno Oliveira admitted to making "countless errors in the training of literally thousands of horses. Luckily I am aware of these faults, for otherwise I would never have made further progress." Even Alois Podhajsky sighed early in his career: "I think I better give up riding altogether. I am never going to learn it!"

The moral of the story is: Don't lose sight of the goal, which is to work with your horse in a willing partnership, and don't lose patience. Klaus Balkenhol, coach of the U.S. dressage team, notes: "The feeling of perfect harmony is achieved only for short pieces of time in a riding session. . . . Don't try to force harmony by constantly hunting for it, which will make you ride more mechanically. Rather, focus on feeling your horse and wait for harmony to happen as a result."

tip 101. Sign up for your next show—or not.

If you haven't already committed to a series of shows for the season, the fact that you and your horse survived your first show intact should propel you into making that commitment now. Don't be in a hurry to move up a level. You have a good chance of increasing your score on the tests you have already mastered when you are less nervous and more confident in your ability. And the more confident you are, the more confident your horse will be. The main thing is that you enjoy yourself and be proud of what you and your horse have accomplished.

However, if you really did not enjoy the pressure of riding before a judge and competing against other riders and their horses, don't feel that showing is the only way to mark your success. Remember, dressage has been a competitive sport for a relatively short period of time, and for centuries classical dressage was an end in itself. A good friend of mine owns several brilliant horses and works them at very high levels, but never in the show ring. She enjoys performing for friends, for professionals, and in demonstrations, but the perfect score in a dressage test is not the reason she rides. She works with her horses for the pure joy of pursuing what Nuno Oliveira called the search for understanding and perfection. "Equitation is not a search for success in public and self-satisfaction after some applause; it is not to please at any price judges at a competition; it is the private dialogue with the horse, the search for understanding and perfection." Trainer Eric Herbermann put it another way: "The horses will ever remain our true and ultimate judges; let us always listen to them."

Further Reading

"By reading, riding, and meditating,
great results may be obtained, if there is
true feeling for the horse and provided
the rider's seat is good."

—Nuno Oliveira

Books

Aust, Stephen. *Classical Equitation Simplified.* To the Point Publishing, 2004. A simplified version of classical training methods.

Budiansky, Stephen. *The Nature of Horses: Exploring Equine Evolution, Intelligence, and Behavior.* New York: Free Press, 1997. A fascinating study of the physiological and psychological aspects of the horse.

Crossley, Anthony. *Dressage: The Seat, Aids, and Exercises.* London: Pelham Books, 1988. A concise and very useful discussion of the important aids.

Decarpentry, General. *Academic Equitation.* North Pomfret, VT: Trafalgar Square, 2001 (original edition 1971). A classic handbook summarizing the teachings of the great equitation masters of the past.

Froissard, Jean. *The Education of Horse and Rider* (incorporating *A Guide to Basic Dressage* and *Classical Horsemanship for Our Time).* Guilford, CT: The Lyons Press 2005. A reprint edition of two basic books by a great French master.

Gahwyler, Max. *The Competitive Edge.* Boonsboro, MD: Half Halt Press, revised ed., 1995. A three-volume guide to competing in dressage.

Gray, Lendon. *Lessons with Lendon: 25 Progressive Dressage Lessons Take You from Basic "Whoa and Go" to Your First Competition.* Gaithersburg, MD: Primedia Equine Network, 2003. A good basic handbook for the novice rider.

Henriquet, Michel. *Henriquet on Dressage.* North Pomfret, VT: Trafalgar Square, 2004. A well-illustrated text by a contemporary French trainer.

Herbermann, Eric. *Dressage Formula*. London: J. A. Allen, revised ed., 1999. A good introduction to dressage basics.

Hinrichs, Richard. *Schooling Horses in Hand: A Means of Suppling and Collection.* North Pomfret, VT: Trafalgar Square Publishing, 2001.

Klimke, Reiner. *Cavalletti.* Guilford, CT: The Lyons Press, 1985. A useful book by a great German master.

——. *Basic Training of the Young Horse.* Guilford, CT: The Lyons Press, 2000. Another useful guide.

Kunffy, Charles de. *Training Strategies for Dressage Riders.* New York: Howell Book House, revised ed., 1994. A well-written discussion of a complicated subject.

——. *The Athletic Development of the Dressage Horse: Manège Patterns.* New York: Howell Book House, 1992. A very useful book with valuable suggestions for exercises.

La Guérinière, François de. *School of Horsemanship*. New York: Hyperion, 1999. One of the great equitation classics.

Loch, Sylvia. *Dressage: The Art of Classical Riding.* North Pomfret, VT: Trafalgar Square, 1990. A well-presented and well-illustrated guide for the serious amateur.

——. *Dressage in Lightness*. North Pomfret, VT: Trafalgar Square, 2000. Another useful book by the same author.

Oliveira, Nuno. *Reflections on Equestrian Art*. London: J. A. Allen, 1976. The only Oliveira book available in English; to be considered essential reading.

Pluvinel, Antoine de. *Le Maneige Royal*. New York: Hyperion, 1999. Another classic text.

Podhajsky, Alois. *The Complete Training of Horse and Rider*. North Hollywood, CA: Wilshire Books, 1967. A basic book by the former director of the Spanish Riding School; must reading.

——. *My Horses My Teachers*. Doubleday, 1968. A warm appreciation.

Ruffieu, F. Lemaire de. *The Handbook of Riding Essentials*. New York: Harper and Row, 1986. A very useful and well-illustrated guide to the basic aids.

Russell, Eleanor. *Gymnastic Exercises for Horses the Classical Way*. Sydney, Australia: E&E Russell, 1995. A small but helpful book of exercises.

Schaik, H.L.M. van. *Misconceptions and Simple Truths in Dressage*. New York: Hyperion, 1990. A fascinating book discussing some of the controversial issues.

Stanier, Sylvia. *Art of Lunging.* London: J. A. Allen, 1993. A good, basic guide to a not-so-simple subject.

Swift, Sally. *Centered Riding.* New York: St. Martin's Press, 1985. A modern classic.

Wynmalen, Henry. *Dressage: The Finer Points of Riding.* North Hollywood, CA: Wilshire, 1971. Another modern classic.

Xenophon. *Art of Horsemanship.* Sydney R. Smith Sporting Books, 1999. An ancient classic of the fourth century BC, considered the basis of classical equitation.

Magazines

Two magazines should be considered essential reading for serious amateurs: *Dressage Today* and *USDF Connection.* The first is published by Primedia; for subscriptions, write 656 Quince Orchard Road, Suite 600, Gaithersburg, MD 20878, or e-mail dressage.today@primedia.com. *USDF Connection* is free with a membership in the United States Dressage Federation, 220 Lexington Green Circle, Suite 510, Lexington KY 40503, or visit www.usdf.org.

Acknowledgments

For their help and advice in writing this book, I would like to thank two individuals in particular for encouraging me in both writing and riding—my trainer, Bettina Drummond, and my editor, Steve Price. I am grateful to each of them in more ways than I can count. I would also like to thank those who helped me in my research and in gathering photographs: Mari Austad, Mary Bloom, Tina Cope, Donna Coughlin, Deborah Cybulski, Carol Epstein, Rosalie Harper-Lewis, Lynndee Kemmett, Patricia Kuehner, Harold LaDue, Catherine McWilliams, Barbara Mele, Wendy Murdoch, Gail and Werner Rentsch, and Kate Rudich. And I must also acknowledge the tremendous debt I owe to the great masters whose wise words are included here, although I take all responsibility for the context in which they are used.